I'M A
Sewciopath

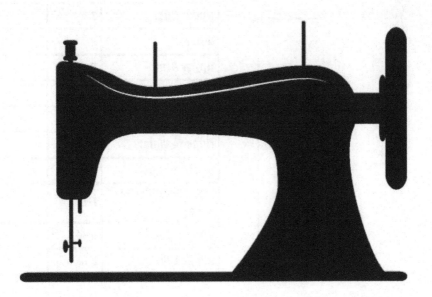

Measurement

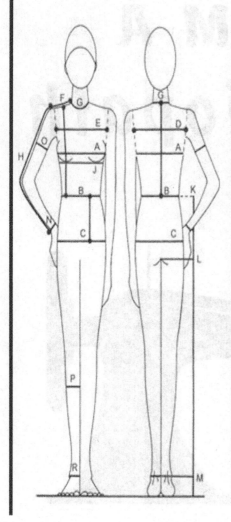

Bust	A	
Waist	B	
Hips	C	
Back Width	D	
Front Chest	E	
Shoulder	F	
Neck Size	G	
Sleeve	H	
Under Bust	J	
Wrist	N	
Upper Arm	O	
Calf	P	
Ankle	R	
Nape to Waist	G B	
Waist to Hip	B-C	
Front Shoulder to Waist	F-B	
Outside Leg	K-M	
Inside Leg	L-M	

MEASUREMENT

Height: Stand with your feet slightly apart and your back against a wall. Have a helper measure from the floor to the tip top of your head.

Bust: Relax your arms at your sides, measure the fullest part of your bust, keeping the tape parallel to the floor.

High Bust: Again, relax your arms at your side and measure just above your breasts.

Waist: Measure loosely around your natural waist. Your natural waist will be between your belly button and your rib cage.

Hips: Measure the fullest part of your hips and back side, making sure to keep the tape level.
Again, make sure to measure loosely.

Rise: Holding the tape at the center back of your natural waist. Run the tape between your legs, pulling comfortably at the crotch, and up to your natural waist in front.

Inseam: Measure from your crotch to the bottom of your ankle. You can also measure the inseam of your best fitting pant to get your inseam measurement.

Arm: Bend your elbow 90 degrees and place your hand on your hip. Hold the tape at the center back of your neck. Measure across your shoulder to your elbow, and down to your wrist. The total length in inches is your sleeve length.

SEWING GOALS

Made in the USA
Coppell, TX
27 November 2024

41133935R00069